Shadow Work
Daniel Warner

Shadow Work
Copyright © 2019
By Daniel Warner
All rights reserved

Cover art: Nicolas Delort
Book design: Daniel Warner
Edited by: Chris West
Printed in the USA

Warner, Daniel
First Edition
ISBN: 978-1-950495-03-0
Library of Congress Control Number: 2019948275

LUCID HOUSE PUBLISHING
961 Bridgegate Drive
Marietta, GA 30068

CONTENTS

I. 7

FISSURE IN THE ENDLESS MAW   8

WAKING UP IN THE MIDDLE OF THE NIGHT TO GO WALKING   9

HAUNT   11

BONFIRE EUPHORIA   13

BONFIRE EUPHORIA II   15

BONFIRE EUPHORIA III   16

JUMPING GOATS   18

YOU SEEM ANXIOUS, YOU SHOULD DRINK SOME MORE COFFEE   20

HEART OF THE THING   22

MATTER BOUND BEINGS   24

WANT VS. NEED   25

INTROVERT'S MELODRAMA   27

SORRY FOR ANY INCONVENIENCE   29

MIDDAY MURDER   31

GILDED FRAME   32

YOU'RE HUNTING FOR UNICORNS AT THE BAR WHEN JACK LONDON WALKS IN   33

DOMICILE OF THE SHIVERING HAUSFRAU   35

WESTERN STARS, EASTERN MOUNTAINS   36

THE LISTENING   37

THE SUBURBAN LAWN   38

II. 41

TIME IS A WIND THAT DOESN'T MOVE AIR   42

ALONE   43

TRACE NO LEAVES   44

DEAR JUNE,   45

EATING BREAKFAST   46

WRENS IN THE WARREN   47

SYMBOLIC LANGUAGE   48

REWILDING   49

III.   50

WALK IN MIDNIGHT RAIN   51

SECOND SLEEP   53

SKY PAINTED WITH LEAVES   56

PEDAL TO THE MEADOW   59

WAYAH BALD   60

IMPENDING GALACTIC DOOM   62

THERE IS A DOG ON ME   64

236 FILE STREET   65

MILLENNIAL DARKNESS AND MAINSTREAM MELANCHOLY   68

ALL YOU HAVE TO DO IS WALK TO THE PORCH   70

SUMMITING RABUN BALD THE FOURTH TIME   72

WELCOME TO THE FOREVER HOLE   74

SCORCHER   75

WHAT'S GOOD   77

THE GOOD MOMENT   78

THESE DAYS I GROAN LIKE AN OLD OAK WHEN RISING   81

NEW YEAR, 2019: CAPTAIN OF THE SADNESS BOAT   82

SUMMER NIGHT   86

MANY ROACHES DROP FROM A POSTER OF VARIOUS PICTURES OF ME DRESSED AS AN ALIEN   88

THE EYES IN WINDOWPANES   90

FLICKING ASHES OFF THE PIER   92

I. SHADOW PEOPLE   94

II. SHADOW WORK   95

III. THE TRUEST REALITY IS THE IMAGINATION   96

DRIVING WEST   97

ORANGE CIRCLES OPEN TO A BIGGER ORANGE CIRCLE   98

LEAVING THE OVEN ON   100

ARRIVING SOMEWHERE   101

SITTING AMONG SYCAMORES, OUTSIDE OF TIME   102

CHARLIE   103

VAGUE APPROXIMATIONS OF THINGS OTHER PEOPLE HAVE SAID BEFORE AND IN BETTER WAYS   105

I.

FISSURE IN THE ENDLESS MAW

I have killed an angry child and opened its wound to the world.

I cast from the second highest branch of mother,
who has become a medium sized oak.
Moonlight in the hair.
Moonlight in the river,
silver slivers.

I used to think what terrified me of open water was the depth
of the unknown.

What is at the bottom
of thought?

What terrific and terrible animals lurk,
too sacred and scared to be seen?

All I wanted was to be seen, to be held by the water.

Wind, a waterless current, breathes into me.

I know this branch will hold.

The wind of my mother breathes through me.

Water restlessly ripples.
Albino fat fish streak in their lunar allure.
I wait for a tug on the line.

Dad is a darkness I am pulling out.

WAKING UP IN THE MIDDLE OF THE NIGHT TO GO WALKING

Towards sunset, in the red pellucidity,
shadows come off our hands.

At night, unmoored by the moon,
she wanders until she finds water.

She lives inside her secrets,
wants to be part of something greater

but doesn't yet know
how to flow against the wake.

And don't we all
want to stretch our shadow
beyond these dreams we clutch?

Ravens swarm from the water and form
a darkness that bends a branch into a beak.

A stampede of wings scatters to claim their trees.

In earlier years, she'd lean against the wind on the cliff
and the air was enough to catch her.

At night, her shadow's shadow
envelops her.

It begins with several white blooms of a few lone magnolias

erupting into magnitudes
of haunting glow.

Then owls announce the hour.

They are the hues of rain drenched bark.

The hemlock spur leans into its gloom.

She breathes in the fullness of morning, and it ends.
There are no shadows and there is no wind.

From an Atlantic apartment, I am dreamed back by the pines;
while in my dreams my mind assembles the self I must wake to.

HAUNT

There are ways we hunt to be haunted.
I am haunted by the places I have been silent.
The words follow me like ghosts:
whispers from mountain water
and sock mildew from last week's rain.

My ego invades its echo, or,
things I wish dad told me:

Streams at different speeds make different sounds.
This is a language you can learn to speak.

If you dissolve into another person,
you do not find yourself.
You have found another person.

If you find what you've been looking for where you first started,
you have found gratitude.
Gratitude is a boundless place.

What torches you into wholeness?
Ashes become a single thing.

I am a city of cells.
I am a database for memories.
I empower plant's inevitable takeover—
which starts with the infrastructure
of sidewalk cracks.

I fight evolution all the time,
and here I am.

I am a hole that is whole.
And still, I can be undone with a single word, which I am grateful for.

I breathe memories.
If you close your eyes,
I can offer them to you.
One day we will be the same ashes.
You will find what you are looking for.
You will find yourself.
You will speak where you've been silent.
You will find the words,

and be haunted by them.

BONFIRE EUPHORIA

I curate silences.
They cloud around me.
In the silence I curate a body.

Our bodies form a mandala
under a tarpaulin sky.
The central fire dances

with our shadows.
The blackness chatters—
raven's beak, crow-caw.

A wristwatch twitches
with its captured insect.
In the bottle we spit

a history of stories.
Numb to numbers,
from our mouths pour

the torpid bathwater of american literature,
and occasionally Rumi.
The great, vapid mobs heave

and we have only seconds left.
Beyond our lit shadows dancing like drunks,
monsters sway. This moment contains

every moment.
Until River's turgid anima speaks
and takes us out of our dalliant shadows.

I leave to find a new silence.
A dragon costume
has swallowed sixteen shirtless people

and circles the holy effigy like a wind
from Jericho.

Absinthe erodes a square into a cup of spicy cold,
and an absence of sobriety.
You act cool and I like you less

but it doesn't matter because we are anchored
by these wine glasses
and their lack of metaphor.

The wandering matador looks at me
and I look for the bull,
but he is waving his cape

and my fingers are horns.
Liquid men move through the liquid night, and mutter:
handsome, Pisces

and hamburger.
I sleep naked under a naked sky.
I wake up

and it is the next day.
I wake up again and it is the next day.
One morning the fire is instead a pile of black earth.

In daylight, the dragon takes the form
of sunburned people walking around a camp.
We scatter like embers on wind,

but the nights stay like tattoos.

BONFIRE EUPHORIA II

Your head is an island in fog.
Crickets in the dark.
Grass folds over itself many times.
Grass touching
is all one thing.
Our upper arms touching
are one thing.
Your head remembered
is lantern lit,
is a matchstick.
You are telling stories to others and laughing.
Fire crackles and embers singe my thigh.
The giant whale in the distance is falling and flaming.
Last night is falling and flaming. We have time,
so we keep saying.

O, how quickly we'll shut the door
as soon as we've looked in.

BONFIRE EUPHORIA III

I don't know what I said but my hands were on yours.

My hands weren't on yours but I wanted them to be.

Fear of joy is the bear in my cage.

I drink wine like you,
lip by lip,
tiny sips.

The wine is both like you and I am drinking it in the way you do.

In this erotic forgetting, we are catching fireflies.

Our childhood's balloons rupture and eruct,
small ribbons in our hands.

Cicada song erupts.
Ribbits. Rabbits.

Foxes snake like a necklace to their den.

I don't know what to do with my hands.
I pick my nails between my questions and your answers.

We tuck our wrists into a pocket
of the universe.

Words drag along like days.
I miss the ground that right now I am on.

You don't see the wars I wage under my skin.

I access reality by imagining it.
I crab walk in the dim din.

We know so little of ourselves.

The negative of your face in the pillow
kisses the back of my head,

but I can't turn to face it.

JUMPING GOATS

What brings us here
to this century?

The barely audible mumblings from the TV men's mouths?
The promise of warm chicken fetuses?
This dirt water is a drinkable temperature.
Please return it to scorching.

My political gesture is avoidance.

The brew percolates beneath the rhythm of voices,
some excited, some held back.

Something dark is brewing.
French roast.

A day old brine watches from the top of pitcher
a hand puts back to deal with later.

Bitterness is a thin skin indeed.

True I should probably stop pirating shows,
and there is a cake of dust on most ceiling fans

If you put your hand out of a moving car,
the resistance is like the warm press of person.

Not that I would admit I get lonely sometimes,
and the empty chair opposite me seems like an expectation.

People get up and go.
Someone cleans the mugs and wipes what would feed many birds.

Other faces replace the ones behind the counter.

The emptying cup is like a question.
Shadows on the street lengthen slowly like hair.
And why are we here?

Down the road a mile, a culvert gurgles with this nonstop rain
that pours like an endless cup of coffee.

As we slowly kill the oxygen in this room,
someone opens the glass door
and another year swooshes in.

YOU SEEM ANXIOUS, YOU SHOULD DRINK SOME MORE COFFEE

The black morning wakes into a row of crows on a wire.
A body rustles a blanket of newspapers,
blends with the bricks.
There would be silence
but the mind is so
so loud.

Cucumbers cross sectioned
and a corset-esque chemex set
set brief, moody shadows
in the window's hypotenuse.
How wordy our not-hearing.

Blueberries mull in a large mason jar.
They sweat sweetly and gleam
in the slant sunbeam—
the architect of shadows
playing on the tiles. Lemons
glisten in translucent infusion—
listen to the minutes' profusions,

which stretch like a sleek cat in the cafe's half light.

The years pour over bagged dirt from a middle latitude.

We are connected by the land,
and pretend that there is a plan.

How would-be our not here-ing.

The hungry nose of the vacuum
snorts what the barista tosses
from the grief of her life.

She cries tiny knives and, falling,
they unzip the mystery
of her worldview—

which is mostly 7 people
and a series of popular,
forgettable songs.

Have I mentioned I'm sorry today?

How woody the knotted clearing.

I am the city and the woods.

I am the skeletal winter of Wisconsin.

I am the body across the street.

I am the Stop sign inverted in the puddle
and the neon sign loading its O.

I'll never be enough.

I've forgotten the easy prayer—
which is hard, warm clay in the hand.

HEART OF THE THING

The next life is no place to enter.
There obliterates.
Here I am already.

In coffee's black surface, dad looks back.
Thoughts enter my now
like bright koi and, as coyly,
scatter.
The coffee coils.

A mud serpent leaps and devours me into its deluge.
Simple stream and endless dark.
No stars but faint light.
Standing knee-deep in the rush,
water swift as souls of the undamned desperate for the dark—
death draws water in a rusted pail.

It has no physical body
and is made of the space around it.
Guided by neither duty nor leisure,
its patient movements are humanlike.
The river moves like time over what would be toes.
Silence connects us.
It takes the pail and turns,
light going with it.

The darkness is total and annihilating,
but familiar.

This is the heart.

A sound from my chest,
slow and booming.
A sound from everywhere at once,
booming and slow.

A neon flash — a far off future —
shines it teeth,
accelerating as the water rises.
The light is obliterating and beautiful
and the river is red with dead fish.

Zeppelins, elephantine and numberless
enter what was darkness.

I ring the seventh leather-strapped silver bell from my belt.

A moment opens my mouth like a door
and shoves its hand in
and I'm not depressed anymore.
I have also learned to lie about it.

Someone asks me how I'm doing,
and I have no answer.

Ripples in the coffee look like dimples.

The heart of the thing is my thought of the heart of the thing.

MATTER BOUND BEINGS

Human shaped light on silvered glass
shrugs where it shoulders tension, settles in

to the matter of its body.

And what to say about the matter
of the body?

The self is what is not
occupied by the body.
The body is separate

from the matter around it.

Here the viewer and the viewed,
in nude immateria, view one thing.

There, a shadow of truth
selves in an absence.

Where the shadow and mirror meet
a third likeness is thricely selved
in absence embodied by shadow.

The body, as perceived from within,
moves in relation to the one.

Shadows of the mind rise early to drink morning,
passing the body's reflections,
to comfort the creature they're housed in
before returning to the dream of sleep,

where the creature roams the knowledge of the heart's homely deep.

WANT VS. NEED

A swipe, a match, and a few snaps at 5 am.
Now you're checking in to a psych ward.

You have a kid. Two.
And some bruises.
But who isn't kidding?
But whose ego isn't bruised?

Still, I find a way to make this about me.
And my stupid crow's feet.

Caw caw you have unbalanced shoulders.

You say you know what you want and I don't believe it.
Another me thing.

But what a gift it is to read.
What a gift to read the stars—

is something I'd like to want to say.

Instead I'm trying to light my brain on fire with a small rectangle.
I'm a fly on a string tethered to your phone's
front facing camera.
It doesn't feel right

to do anything.

My 'why' trails behind me
and maybe that's where it belongs.

I want to say things less and feel things more.
But let me run away first.

When Aubrey looks at the camera I lose it.

I don't know what IT is anymore and I've lost IT.

I want it to rain lightly and I want a porch.

I want to be a candle in your darkness.
I want to be your question and I don't want an answer.
I want to not want anything.

Want is a language I've made.
I want to live and nothing more.
I want my hand held in the rain.
I want that to not sound stupid.

My language will not blow your mind,
but you will know it immediately. It will be
a place of safety.

I say too much.
Let's walk barefoot in the wet
and learn a different way to speak.

The white lights on the high floor of the ward
echo in my mind as afterimages. In all living, I live alone.
And all I am asked to do is breathe.

I am alone and around others.
In the long line down the hall, there is one
beneficent silhouette after another.
They all live and breathe and smile
and I sink into the floor.

I am not what I asked for.

INTROVERT'S MELODRAMA

Rolling green fields of wild apathy.
Chaos of the unseen breeze,
and the stillness after.

The flag waves.

A symbol of hope and war catches an air current
but is terrestrially tethered
by a piece of metal shoved into the ground.

You don't have to put your hand on your heart
during nationalist propaganda,
though socially it is advisable.

You can choose to not dance when others are dancing.
Presence holds more power than words.

Dancing in 2019 is sexual undulation.
It's a mating ritual, a primal thing.

What if you lean into the primal thing instead of resisting it?

Make wub in the club.
Dance if you want to.
You can leave your friends behind.

You can think about robots during the allegiance pledge
and scan the room for recording devices if you want to.

You can wear your hood that
nullifies the orgasmic bass.
You *are* a dinosaur.

Eat the cat.
Words are cheap, so boil your friends

and wear your enemies' skins.

Hang out on rooftops at night
and stir your cauldron.

Let your mind wander
but don't be surprised when it brings back an absent male
role model's spine.

Lean, lean into the wind.
Turn your back against the cold.
Come as you are.

Oh, we've been waiting for you.

SORRY FOR ANY INCONVENIENCE

I hear the soul in its box
floating to some unknown end
down this road that winds through the Pisa airport
and back around to Galileo's house.
I smell how long it's been

since I've gotten a haircut.

I can tell each car is vacant at this hour.
Mostly an assumption, based on the silence
of hatchbacks ubiquitous in this city—so welcome
a lowering in nightly volume to trucks
that I panic, not knowing what to do

with all this quiet.

So I pour an extra glass and pour it out.
So I walk a fence around the bed.
So I strip the bed and lie on the floor.
So I float through the ceiling
into the open maw of space

and destroy my sense of self entirely.

I can feel the A/C's grumble before I hear it.
Stale air first fills its mechanical lungs,
then it realizes it must share with the whole room
if it is to condition at all.
Each whoosh I think might be rain

and am mistaken.

But maybe they're not true, the things we say
in the quiet hours of our self-slanderings.

Second canceled flight this week,
and my mind is full of sandwiches
with too much bread.

One day I will sleep

and believe that I have rested.
I will wake up, and that will be enough.
For now I will crumble
this thin ticket that says
Complimentary Drink Voucher,

and I will eat it.

MIDDAY MURDER

"Flap flap, bitch," the crows seem to say in passing.

Einstein's head floats in unsubmerged delay
behind the boat's stern carving.

What absence, what lack draws me to the black
of the crows? Earlier the answers ran

by and wore neon soles but my gaze stopped
at the barefoot beaver feeder, whose wrist is twirled inward.

He plays Euro-trash techno and feeds the green-
headed geese expired fruit

fresh from behind the store.
He also feeds the beavers

who meet him at the edge of the water.
They retreat at the sound of the kid's cycle

catching in the grooves of the wooden bridge.
Ducks race the kayak sprinter and pass him

when his shoulders relax in slowing.
For a second, I inhabit the space of a crow's eye

as it flies by. Such a breeze might carry me home.
I lift my wings, but they are only arms.

GILDED FRAME

The thumps of hooves shake the morning loose.
The cat in the alley is gone with dawn.
You shut the curtains but don't wish for rest.
The soft blue of morning coalesces
felinely. A shadow in the corner
of the snowed-in street is a horse painting
war with red eyes. The art hung on your wall
depicts this: man, horse, snow, red snow, and a
gilded frame with the exact same painting.
On the hunched back of the world, soft blue snow
slushes from cars and hooves and feline prints.
What I'm saying is this: you must learn to walk
in the world. The horse and his creepy teeth
did. You must look in the mirror and do
yoga. Then you literally can't be
sad. Let your spine crack like lightning as you
assume the shape of a scorpion. What
I mean this time is: the future is here.
The past's also here. The eternal now
is a book not worth reading. I digress
and the horse is rearing, and blood's been shed.
Crawl out of the life you have been painting.
Be the horse you've always wanted to be.

YOU'RE HUNTING FOR UNICORNS AT THE BAR WHEN JACK LONDON WALKS IN

Your wolf wife starts eyeing Jack London.
You start eyeing Jack London.
You say: *You know he only wrote White Fang,*
he's not the same as White Fang.
She says: *I'm aware*, tapping her front paw.
You sip the dregs of a cheap gin,
 a drop of dead juniper burning its ghost on your tongue.
At the bar, you see he's drinking scotch.
Of course, you think.
And you check your pockets for scotch money.
You look back at your wife.
So? She asks with her eyes.
You shrug: *We have a problem.*
She rolls her eyes,
then folds her arms.
Well?

You order another cheap gin,
at the last second turning toward Jack.
Hey, are you-
Busy? He looks to you with the scotch at his lips.
He finishes it off and slams it on the table.
You jump a little.
Look, I know what's going on here.
You turn completely around to face him. *Really? How-*
Happens all the time.
He blinks his yellow eyes.
I'm flattered, really.
You scratch your head with your wolf arm: *So-*
But I'm chasing other tail tonight.

Jack pours another scotch, slams it on the bartop
and walks over to a pack of wolf girls
trying to leave a table of loud frat boys.

He bears his white fanged grin and they smile
all open mouthed and giddy,
wrapping their arms around his.
He looks back at you still sitting at the bar
and winks as they walk away into a sleepless night.
For a second your eyes grow wide and you worry your wife is with them,
but she is at the bar on your other side. She puts her hand on your knee.
She's ordered a bottle of scotch and, before you can object,
she's holding a glass of it in front of your face.

On me.
You hold her amber gaze a moment,
then take the glass.
Fucking writers, you mumble as you tip back the scotch.
Shards of peat and sea foam lodge into your throat from that first sip.
And she pours you another.

By the seventh glass, the burn is the burn of a soft fire
and your faces are so close they make the silhouette of an hourglass.
You have no idea what you've been talking about,
but every word has been perfect.
Every word a story that hasn't yet been written.
The bar is closing, and you take the empty bottle home as a trophy,
falling asleep half naked in the den tangled up in each other.
Eventually your hand relaxes, the bottle rolling away
and stopping at the wall.
Your wolf arm is still wide awake and it howls at the yellow moon,
four distant howls echoing in return.

DOMICILE OF THE SHIVERING HAUSFRAU

Sylvia, shivering hausfrau,
searched for peace in a deep and private present,
seeking the face on the other side.
She followed its form into the real,
and baked her way into domesticity,
looking for a way out by looking in.
One day gardening, a thought planted in her.
Something broke and something opened up.
The sun was low and cast long shadows.
Heiligenschein as her hair entered first.
Scent of animalia carried through the kitchen.

*Composed from lines of Sylvia Plath's poems and interviews

WESTERN STARS, EASTERN MOUNTAINS

I wade into the quiet of the stream
lost in isolated absolution of absolute isolation.

On the mirror of the blazing dynamo of stars,
the moon sings a harmony.

Time is a liquid like the mirror of selvings
unfolding in the ablution of waves

folding over waves of now
folding over waves of the here.

Do you hear it?
The singing. The ringing

moon. Water and what are
self in the folds of time's gloss and sheen.

I suspend in the multitude of selves,
drifting in that oneness of uterine night.

I press into that death. I lay into its depths.
What primal memory carries the wave onto my skin?

Why only see the negative?
Why see that as negative?

Does this makes sense?
You make up sense.

THE LISTENING

There will be a simple tale well told,
when our lives come around to it.
Single tree in a snowfield.

Birds will scrawl three taloned prints on the blank page of snow.

The story will be deep as the chasms of the heart
next to the old wounds.
East to life and west to death.

The blooded sun hangs sharply
on the morning's thorn.

The barn door is listing and blows back and forth without regard to time.

A rusty truck rages by hurtling to doom the dim faces lit blue
by the viewing screens of their boxes.

They round the curve with crates of beagles in the back,
and come back with only crates.

Their mouths on the windows make no sounds.

Along the seven mile road,
the truck is the only thing moving

except for the branch full of crow's hungry eyes.

THE SUBURBAN LAWN

Bird shit cakes windshields and bumper plates.
Gutters gurgle from last night's rain.
It is the hour before the sun's tongue.
Before the television is on
telling its vision of new.
Though, there is nothing new
on the television, save a few
fingerprints from its recent mounting.
A mountain of boxes makes a lean-to
against the brick facade of the landing,
where a mother repeats phantoms of a Prom scene-
corsage, boutonniere, and car bumper speckled white.
The porch buzzes electric blue in the swell of grass's
hidden symphonies. More boxes spill into the quiet green expanse
of suburban lawn.
A Mark Doty line pops into mind as a child's head
emerges from a well
manicured bush.
The child disappears
like a popped balloon,
and another floats on a plank of wood before school
in the amniotic fluid of a red sky morning.
O tear in the heat of summer
through which blue bullets rain.
It is this heat through which hopes hopscotch
hot and heavy like a first kiss
set to Coldplay. Tony Hawk will have kids
of his own by now, and will feel the presence
of geese and other bird droppings on the stagnant toilet called a bird
bath that pushes down on the grass
that never stops pushing up.
He will be asked what he is up to nowadays
by cashiers and flight attendants and he will say
"This."
A boy-in-a-hoodie hawks a Lugia
from a younger boy-in-a-hoodie's pocket of monsters.

Teenagers roll their ankles under the pear tree
that reaches up to their open windows at 2 am, the time
when the eyes in the back of mom's head turn out.
Two teenagers emerge from a Firebird's closed trunk, smoke rising.
Where do they go in their cold metal?
In the labial folds of depressive years,
hair is cut and gelled, and sheets go unwashed.
Boxes pile and the paint yellows.
Let us go then, and walk this half mile loop
for then we will be happy.
Let us not speak of the affairs of the gutters
or of the narrow space between houses
of today and tomorrow.
Here in this half light the children show
the younger children how to shoot the bird.
The years grow longer and close together
like grass slowly retaking a yard.

TOO HIDDEN OR TOO EXPOSED?

1.
Water trails its tail. The acid dark drops.
A southern and slow drawl of wind ripples the dark surface.
The wind a language you could almost hear.
Its tales hang musky and vaporous, humid and languid.
Vapor's fingers absorb effusive light.
The human tall, bright green grass still bends to the flow.
The stream, serpentine, winds into the hill.
Pinecones open in the rain.
There is a sound you can almost hear.
Here. Wade into the quiet of the stream.

2.
The sun rose rose.
In the red light, found a way to rest with the darkness.
Setting suns of several days dotted an ellipse.
Between the hills' held light, it was valley sunny.
And then the eclipse, slow as honey.
The afternoon closed its eye, and shadows of birds
joined the one shadow.

II.

TIME IS A WIND THAT DOESN'T MOVE AIR

Emptiness,
inner wilderness, look!
The morning came.
It is all around us.

And separate things
like crow and water
and image of crow on water
are not really separate at all.

The transparent stillness of this moment
where nothing is different,
is the portal through which time moves.

Which is how the river moves,
and how the crow in the river moves.

Look,
the morning is here!
Let us participate in the disintegration.

ALONE

The clock tower drums time
with distant hands.
The sun, blood orange,
buries this waking in a hazy shimmer.
Age old ego blazes.
The last church's spire reflects
in high rise window glass.
Glockenspiel figurines barely keep their noses above the water.

Goofy pitches the bone oar and it catches with a thump on a floating body.
He pushes off from the bloated thigh,
which totters on its axis.
The lamp swings in the coiling fog.
The current swills in the wake of his push;
a calligraphy of smoke.
The canoe glides out over the water
Goofy smiles with his teeth,
for he is finally alone.

TRACE NO LEAVES

Chickory smoke
spices air sliced
by barren hemlock
branches, Maxwell House
and Folger's cans collecting rust
from braided twine against the peeling bark
of the forgotten pine scent
since sent backwards down wind-
ing backwood roads
to the Dollar General
where a coarsely unshaven man
shake shake shakes his tin can hoping for change
in the generally dolorous haze of Georgia
where wildflowers turn to wildfires
in the changeless, unquenchable
scorch of June's shade.

DEAR JUNE,

When the midday sun was setting
I broke a tree and cut my leg watching a lizard
and fell into the black hole of you,
soul's red light seeping.

Pins of light thread through night
as beetles eat through green, writhing
warmth rising to cool the swarming fever.

I think I only feel safe surrounded by water.

Shadows sweep
across the silence,
stretch into peripheral bats.

Night needles in with spider bites.
In sleepless fits of rolling,
the mountains hold their heat.

I sweat in the swelter,
my body not fit for the earth.

A snake coils partially underground,
lifts its head to catch the breeze.

Geese pull the cord of sunlight,
splinter the dark room of heaven
with birdsong.

EATING BREAKFAST

In the kingdom by the sea, bone
white beaches are strewn with garbage.

Night knits its archaic cage with cicada song.

A whippoorwill beaks a cigarette
and brings it to his nest.

The window slices clear
a distance between my sight
and my seeing.

The rush of water soothes.

The wind howls at nothing all dark long.

The moon, a white fang,
journeys to the sky's end—
which is a book turning to its first page.

The hour's shadow looms large.

Cereal pours into the landfill of you.

The bones of yesterdays burn in your engine so you can sit in a box.

WRENS IN THE WARREN

The sky sheer fabric of the blue unreal slips
diaphanously down.

In the aerial sleep,
the stars tooth in.

The cedar branch's ash hovers on its smoke,
and is its ghost.

The starry night's mind that wraps the world is like the cave of a skull,
blank and full of animal imagery.

You think how thin the separation between the space of your body
and the body of space.

The ancient surge of stars breathe in and out
in their mute and stellar incantations.

Pale stars hang on their threads,
lingering like the last cedar cinders smoldering.

Walk out of the stars and into the grass.
Let the morning sun's red rinse wrench you from the mind's water.

In the deep winter of yourself, find a way to make meaning
of the meaninglessness.

SYMBOLIC LANGUAGE

I am a region of joylessness.
For joy first enters an emptiness.

Then flowers beyond a feeling.

Black is not the void.
Black is night,
which is bloated with stars.

In place of a soul,
there is the constant cold
departure.

Void as inner room.
There is no moon.

There is only the waiting space of my mouth for the word,
shaped like a moon.

Not the great pair of wings skimming their mirror.
Not the world spinning and sloshing its water,
but what the words evoke in the witness.

Trees, breeze, unstilled water.

Remove names,
and things are just things.

People are parts
of the landscape.

Are questions more important than their answers?

REWILDING

Sleep hangs above me like the wings of a dream.
The river runs in and through me.
Tiny suns in eyes open to larger suns.
Southing doves fly as one wing over the hill and into the sun.
I breathe them in.
The dead things hurt most but that dies down.
An acorn, in the random rain of acorns,
opens in the rain.
Time arcs across the distances of the sky and I,
looking through the clouds and not at them,
see all versions of myself seeing what I want to see
and not what I am.
What is a person but a heap of broken images?
I will become something greater than a notion
motioning at itself in the dark.
A stream carves its path and trickles away.
Wings tilt against the world's turning.
Mottled bloom of moon hangs in wing's wake.
In the eddy where the riptides meet,
the sun is fractured and submerged.
This is not hope, it is a trail.
Years pass like slow suns setting into themselves.
The wings cascade in the gully of the wind-shaped hillside.
The bud opens its flower to the world.

III.

WALK IN MIDNIGHT RAIN

We are all our phantom fathers after a while.
I withhold so much from the world—
hoarding like Smaug.

How much do I have
to reorder words before they are new again?
Is poetry just translating old ideas
into the parlance of the time?

Not enough rain for the umbrella,
so I shoulder it like a rifle.
Firefly in the city.
Just one.

The cynic in me wants to snuff it in my hand until I realize
how deeply I'm breathing.

And how many things are excuses to breathe—
cleaning, running, sweeping,
sleeping, seeping into.

Parking lot lingerers loiter,
litter, leave. A litter with kittens
enjoys a box by the padlocked ice chest.

I'm done crushing experience into bite sized bits.
Everything seems a miniature of itself—
tilt-shifted. I stare at a page and not its words.
I notice it's raining in the ghost glint
of a green leaf. I take a walk

to have an experience.
My shoes are a barrier to feeling
so I take them off. The puddle obscures the ground
and I sit in it. I am sodden,

so I move through the streets like a dream.
Every image a symbol for something else,
like a word instead of its thing.
And how many poems will it take?

I am writing back to the center.

A year ago I walked in the mist
wrapped mountains and fell open,
and I've never quite come back.

SECOND SLEEP

1.
Winter groans low and lonely from the belly of the cave.
The valley bellows below, groans for the lovely green of spring,
in mute and hidden solace like a star, dreams beyond its lifetime's deep
wintering.

At the intercession of celestial interstices, in the corner
of the frozen water's gleam, history's crossing winds
efface the present. The cool current of self
rinses all former selves, redeems past trespasses
and rends the meaning of time.

I see regret, gazing the greyblue horizon.
I see egrets inside the sun, now out.
I move in time's wash, where wind breathes across the breadth.

The egrets' triangular triumvirate greets me from the north.
I believe them for they do not use words.
Their song is long and their sleep will be deep.

The river stones stutter in their shallow parley, in dream.
This waking, it has been said before, is like a sleep.
Where winds meet above water's murmur, moving in one direction,

where wings flash flying through the yellow iris, I,
domed by rhododendron branches' cursive embracings
drink sun and sink in thinklessness.

2.
Struggle of eyelid in waking to sun.
Tiny orange suns foreshadow the opening
of the lid to the real, the abstract

nowness of new knowledge opening into a pale pink band

of cloudlessness, ending as an indigo ceiling
through which the stars could speak.

These distortions come to seem the natural way of things.
Looking from the outside and craving the within.
Bending the inward through the outward's gleam.

Emptiness extends itself like the sun through clouds,
reaching through time. History a series of words
remembered unhurried and out of order.

How long for this mere breathing and enduring?

3.
I float the months between travel, nearly now
a year since leaving the apartment. There is nothing
new to say, in poetry, in speech.

It takes a foreign country
to navigate the foreign quiet of a heart,
surrounded by a language that is not its own.
There is a scream in silence that lets no one in.
Tonight there will be no sleep.

Metal petals spin on plaster starred sky of ceiling.

4.
Night's petals open.
The sun has turned its back.
The black swirls its glass.

Light's flash dims focus
to a dense point.
Night's indigo flows

back. Stars spread out, colloidal.
Horizon's nadir is Arcturus, from where I still stand.

I can't tell the night from the back of my hand.

Pines' pikes are ghostly and skeletal.
They stab the sky where bright eyes look through:
mythologies to pass the time.

The wind has felled a colossus of pine.

5.
Deep blue space above sky blue water.
The stream pulses under its transparent skein.
A sparse crowd of pine faces the water.

From the imagined sieve,
the membrane of now and then
wavers thin as a feather twirled in the hand.

A cell tower masquerades as natural
among the pines' towering loom—
a Minecraft cactus pretending it's real.

The sun sears a seam where eyes were set.
Where now the eyes are setting.
And I will come here yet

again, and take a feather from the thaw
to later turn and turn,
in vision beyond vision,

which keeps my stray parts whole.

SKY PAINTED WITH LEAVES

1.
Dark's shadow is the light it wraps around.
Sun's shadow covers the ground.
I sit in the leaves and listen.

Fireflies light the night in pulses.

Sometimes I imagine twisting people around
until the faces of their feral ghouls show.

The ghost voice of an absent father follows me
like wind through pines.

I put the voice to sleep
by sleeping too much.

The shadow moves while the body rests.

The old man in the youth's skin
is pulled inside out—
the self is its own cancellation.

There is a hole in the light where dark seeps through.
This is how you know there is light at all.

2.
The darkness of the self behind the mask is lost in fear of its beginning.
The darkness in these sentences is in the words and the sputtering—
the defensive deflections of the heart in fear and search of itself.

Dark's mask hung the clouds of the sky to dry.

There is a hole in the light where darkness seeps through.
There is a hole in the dark where light seeps through.

Shall I rip and rise from this monstrous flesh,
or is this what it means to be human?
The shadows move.

Sit in the dirt of yourself.
Lift off your skull and walk the insides of the earth.
Step in the footsteps pressed by so many others' feet.
Step beyond them.
Step out of memory and into the grass.

I walk through the holes in dark's mask of sun
and emerge next to a pine and its whispering.

The essential darkness shrouds the essential self.

3.
Aureole of white moonlight stands next to reaching pines.
The etched ink image of a body unravels again in the wind—
the dark words slow in the dark woods.

Murmurs of starlings in the moonlight.

A wing of a hundred wings flaps unflappably
up the column of pale fire and soon
is the echo of clouds echoing into rain
echoing into rain.

The analytical sun bears no mask,
or so it seems. This is the dark's mask of self:
a scattering of ink for verbosity's chambering.

A lone bee wakes by falling from its branch
and wing-stilling itself mid-air. And thus
its ceaseless buzzing thoughts begin,
and commit themselves to the discord.

The present mind

in its absent-mindedness
presently forgets the mind's absences—
the shadow unbreaks the breaking that makes you whole.

I provide these frames for shattering the reflection shadowed
in the frame of the inked self's inner seeing.

I dissolve in ink and blend
with the sounds

of the earth
and the spinning
of the pines.

PEDAL TO THE MEADOW

Ghosted again against the glass,
I feel a number of things I interpret as sad.

Meg, you have my same haircut.
Lucie, how many heart necklaces do you need?

The evening's shadows are long and gray.
In the dim light I find a way to rest with the meaninglessness.

I need to learn to appreciate ephemerality
but holy shit that will be short lived.

Other Meg, "wanna pedal to the meadow"
is a question I can't refuse, so here's your poem—
but what meadow did we agree on?

A long body ghosts into the metro, a snakelace around its neck.

In the chaos of strongest feelings, I tend to smile and feel nothing—
ghost Patrick Swayze handling pottery without another person.

And I've seen ghostlier things than these,
watching evening stretch from the afternoon
in this meadow I've pedaled to.

Crown of the setting sun means a quick finish of this pilsner
and back to the hotel.

God damn moon, I'll lasso you down
along with these elusive moments.

WAYAH BALD

Red coal raises in its morning blaze,
melts the frost and glints the dew, goldening

the lines of written harvest. Who am I kidding,
I am in Atlanta.

I forgot my watch in the Tuesday morning rush.

Time without a watch.
It was a time without. A time within.

Have we caught up with where we just were?

Should, must, have to, didn't, should have—
thoughts betray me as soon as I wake.

Days are a processional of shoulds and oughts,
growing in percussive ferocity. I should learn to stop.

Could. Chloe says that even rain in your hair can be an offering.
Thoughts like the white lights in a psych ward's high floor

promise clarity but are blinding and unnatural.
Fall happens and, in a letter from Melissa,

I read her line "to fight the physical limitations of being"
and sit for long moments in my mind thinking about it.

Pines cones fold into batons. Basswood, oak,
and black locust hill. Red eye briefly through the leaves.

The ridge called Wayah Bald will become an apartment
porch in one week's time. The switch will have many thoughts.

Fall's coming appears as a leaving.
The shoulds' muscling,
the crepuscular trees' rustling
raise calamity and calm owls startle into waking.
Scent of birch or pine, yellow or white?

The deluging forwardness of the wind on the hill
engulfs me and I blow like a leaf through the cold,
golden world. Now winter.

IMPENDING GALACTIC DOOM

1.
Into the creek's silver backwardness,
glimpsed glints of Time in age's folds.
Suspended fear of impending galactic doom,
let reason needle down through slats of stacked slate
to weathering gurgle of reality in the stream's forward flow
through its burden of rocks, out of which bent fish like clarities leap.

Have we climbed clear of our wrong beginnings?

2.
Beyond Jones Creek's lush resonance,
spheres of progressively diminishing beauty
hill the horizon, following the flow
of the mountain spring's downward beckoning.

From higher up, the seen
takes on qualities of the seer.

A small brushfire takes on qualities of the orange
above it.

3.
The darkly deep, longly
steeped in red.
A belt of pearls strewn about.
Some know this heaven as their life,
and this frame for their real.
I see the bird holding up the tree.
I see the world pulling its gold chain.

There is a vast death inside.
Am I what is not around me?

4.
In spring, when the separate components of the tree
flame into one single thing, the katydid will brood
under the droop of its dew drop hat leaf.

The summer sleeps beyond these glimpses of winter heat.
The sun unwinds from the tree's logs,
its critters scattering.

A man I've called father
mowed a woman half his age's lawn
and set the apartment alight.

Bearded in the flame of his invective,
eyes red behind smoke he breathed out,
he defended that he had called the fire department.

Inhale: Everything is temporary.
Exhale: Peace.

Sway of the river of tall grass.
The stillness after.

A tree's shadow walks the field
over an afternoon.

Grief's ghosts haunt in circles,
like fanged faces in the distance.

I'm braiding a dream from the natural world.
I can't believe in anything fully.

THERE IS A DOG ON ME

The grass is green under the eave of green leaves.
The blue of the sky is the blue of the pond.

White ivory shines beneath brown bark.
Aphids in silence wage war under bark.

Ants approach my leg from the left.
Your head rests against my thigh.

The column of ants, Georgia clay-red,
seems to extend backwards
into eternity.

I am aware of my lack
of breathing.

Your breath is light,
is fluff and cloud,
and is the anchor

of this deathless summer afternoon.

Our lives are one continuous breath,
and the circle of this peace

creates itself. The sky below is a tinge of green.
The green circles of your eyes surround.

And one day we will hold only memories.
For a moment, I don't need to know why

the sky is all around us.

236 FILE STREET

1.
In wince from eye-flinch of watch's solar ricochet,
witnessed the coming closer, then moving away
of the day from the merely verbal association
made of calf and calf, watching expressionless gnash of cud-chew
not unlike grind of burger chew.

The calves flex and tighten in the same way a calf might, glimpsed,
moon and calves flashing between stalks of
whatever local flora I want to pretend to name.

The images do become the same.
All this under the parabolic curved cloud canopy.
Our stories unfold under the sun.

2.
Earth spins and it is a map of curves
to run one's hands along and uphill.

From the curves is a music and a gyrating of the hips to
and fro like chewing in a lower jaw's undulation.

In moonlight lightning's false flash, peeks of peaks held the sounds of the
previous night's panting recollected in delicious delirium.

In the moment between flexion, in the pull back
before foot kisses earth, there is an invitation.
There is vulnerability. Then the tension returns.
Arithmetic flashes in these connections' conscious conjuring.
That I try in vain now to recollect.

26 years for bearing the fruit of myself. And I pull back.
I cannot be the flower I offer to the world.

The under-music, as of a planetary music box turning,
or a low radio's just imperceptible vibrations,
of the engine's torqued punching punctuates
the glare of the dream
in which these images meet.

3.
What we see and what we think.
The image and the thought of the image.

The word and the sound of the word.
World and sound of world.
The act and thought of the act.
Are not things in the world.

The past now passes into the now.

How do I turn *what has passed*?
Into *what now*?

Now I rewrite the inaction
as an act of collecting
the image into a thought of the image
to recollect when sifting the detritus of memory.

The westering moon
lavishes white
secondary definitions
to undulating lines of field brush
moved by the same wind
that bows towering pines.
The watery white
is like a dream.

Kept in the heart's deep home,
the November day,
wrapped in gossamer sleep,

carries me to dream
in the car's backseat.

The timepiece shifts
a piece of time.
Time's peace shifts.
A long hand pushes one notch forward.

Even in the undoing of these thoughts,
the evening has undone its starry belt.

MILLENNIAL DARKNESS AND MAINSTREAM MELANCHOLY

When you ask questions of others
you're questioning yourself.
My hair is a year past my mouth.
Two ice cubes in my coffee.
The espresso looks into the sun without squinting.
The sunflower field is the same as sunlight.
The heart unfurls only when it wants.
You cannot force this.
Romance is fire on a distant shore.
Heat that you imagine
and that you can feel.
Of course this coffee is not
a romantic gesture.
Romance is dead.
Lamps that swing on windy nights,
oak barn doors that creak.
Images that walk in moonlight
beyond their words; old
hypnosis of the creek. These are the things
in my station wagon. Thoughts
creep like days from bush to bush.
Snails move, lit by stars,
toward mushrooms and dawn.
You'll drown in the thought of love
before reaching the shore of love.
Snails, like the last evening bus at 2am.
Your time is fragile in my hand.
Seeking heaven in the suck of a blunt,
you will likely miss this snail.
The sun drops and mosquito wings fill the night.
Bees gorge on pollen, covered to their knees.
The animals are creating a language
and it's hard for me to be around people.

So I lock myself in the house and rain
comes in the middle of my shame.
Man's genius emanates from his wounds.
The world emanates from its wound.
World wound.
And I from it.
And that which is you
is only a word
scorched in summer.
Will you bow to the heart where it's at?
Romance will come bigger than dreams
booming from the clouds.
A pile of wet logs examines my life.
Rain drums the roof impatiently,
follows its flow
to groundedness.
I wish the meaning
of our plans could be more than clouds.

ALL YOU HAVE TO DO IS WALK TO THE PORCH

The word friend and I lately
have become estranged
and words themselves
seem dispersed
as if underwater.

I am more often in my mind
than the world.

I have this impulse
to use grandiose words
to touch and to name
and so I text slowly.

And so the words, like friends,
are in different places.

Touching a map in two different countries
to see how far the space is between fingers

might be something like this.
The map is in my head.

There is no failure
in not trying.

I withhold.

I bring coffee to the noisy porch
and fail to meditate,
seeking a fluid unity
of mind and body.

I sit with my thoughts and let them speak.

I let the water speak its falling.

I feel it pool under my toes like the Atlantic.

I'll let my mouth do the listening.

I'll walk into the day and not call it anything.
So I say.

SUMMITING RABUN BALD THE FOURTH TIME

Coral colored neurotoxic death snakes
hurry to water, west and downhill.

Truculent succulents and scurrilous squirrels
rage against the dying of the light,

scurry through the quarry out of the yellow eye's
quarrelsome scrying.

Silver spokes of sunlight scythe
through fog-lit clouds' ominous luminosity,

spin the sunset a sinister crimson.
The South's twisted tongue of fire ignites

like magnolia's nocturnal flowerings.
All in beginning is turning, returning

to the central idea. Debauched and deboughed
white pines' towering sway gives

way to windshield wiper blades in Tuesday rain.

Complacency of the anteroom and
the soft light through the window

land gaze to page
and catch the dream.

Furtive gold filaments of the just barely
seen sun setting between oaks in Atlanta

are the same as the gilded glints of Rabun.
The center of the center is nowhere. Now, here.

It is the same wherever I sleep.
When I turn my head,

the page turns with me.
The pines dream me to the center,

and sing from the root.

WELCOME TO THE FOREVER HOLE

I find seeing sadness in other things
pushes the excitement button,

which is connected on the other side
to the abject wretchedness button.

Which is really just seeing myself.

The nicer side of belief is that what you believe might not be true.

What do you believe?

The past lives
in the ghosts of now.

And in phantoms of self-speak.

Let us move into that forgetfulness.

Thought wolf padding water,
it is okay to leave the ocean

for the most great ocean.

Night comes up from the interior
in a motion like sleep.

It hides like stars in daylight.

Is day
the nature of happy?

SCORCHER

I imagine my shoes will melt into this concrete.
It's real hot. Heat wavers everywhere-kind of hot.
There was a moment strolling the sidewalk where the fence
cast a lattice of shadows on my hand
when I wanted to run from shade to shade
as though I had stolen something important, where
hand gridded like a steak,
I noticed the exquisite detail of my creation.

Like when I followed a firefly along a series of obvious trails
branching to less obvious trails
far out of sight of my conflagrant congregation.
The parking lot was nowhere to be found.
All I could do was sit in the dirt of myself and, in the morning,
emerge a mere trail away from snoring naked people.

I'd agree to a baptism in this heat-kind of hot.

O the tension
to scratch the thoughts
is itchy and rough as jumping 100 feet into a pile of hay.

The heat clings to the wet ends of hair.
All the dog's tongues are out.

The people in passing are humanoid absences.

My emotions have been subject to an excess undoing.
With this awareness comes a feverish onslaught of remembering
fully and feeling full.

It's like climbing a ladder that extends through the clouds
into the sky, straight up into space
but without the freezing and the suffocating.

Are we not our memories — and are memories not
a series of locked observations?

The heat is sloth-like and monotheistic.
The summer's persona is a sultry, feline heat.
And this isn't summer.
This is hot stones in your underwear.

Saturn is up there
and what am I avoiding?

A small, locked garden of roses
bloom to their deaths.
The tree rings carry experience
but do they carry knowledge of the experience?

A breeze from nowhere is like a glass water
still and cool, wavering as a mirage.

The giant blue cat's tails blow and blend with the ice blue wind.

WHAT'S GOOD

We express our brilliance only when we express it to each other.
And thus it is hard to know what is good.
When I try to sleep, my eyes bore holes into the ceiling.
The clock ticks years, not hours.

Friend, we have drunk darkness and thus are doomed
to shake it off over the years by walking at night
and avoiding, in particular:
pop music, mint-chocolate chip, yellow, and talk of weather.

We were passing on the street silently
and were at the same time alongside each other like mirrors
howling our insecurities into each other's mouth.
This was the first day of a lifelong friendship.

Now, I walk backward through the house
where the clocks tick in reverse and therefore forward.
This has come to be the familiar way of things.

Too many times I've been too proud to let out what I'm proud about.
But as I've said, we are friends and I wander at night.
But, I fear if we walk at night occupying the same space,
there will only be one of us.
Though we will return to two in the morning.

This is a recurring image to me - two things becoming one
but really being something else from the beginning.

In church, I imagined the pastor being killed in various ways—
chandelier, flying donation plate, falling off the stage,
speaker frequency too high.
Therefore I am unbaptized.

What's good?
What *is* good?

THE GOOD MOMENT

1.
Language is the chasm and the bridge.
I hold back my words.

And yet I show love through language.
For instance, eyelashes

are human feathers.

Some days I want to be a part of redemption.
Some days I want to be a shadow on a dark path.

Sometimes kisses sound like little birds chirping.

I want to think my way to you.
And where is that, exactly?
The good moment,
the beautiful kingdom—
they are already over.
They are a green and red

civilization in my freezer.

I should probably clean that.
Now I want to think my way away from you.

2.
Men make themselves out of their speech.

I'm loving it,
and while I'm sure that's true, love is not
possession of the thing loved,
it's possession of love.

Have it your way,

but the unnatural will not fix the need
for the natural.
Log in to your loneliness alone
and see if that bridges your need for community.

It is the screen of language that mediates the immediate.

And when IG (instant gratification)
fails the deeper needs, you'll go wandering at night
and wonder where wonder went.

And there on the damp lawn will lie your language
coiled in the dark like a question.

3.
Loss grows larger than your body,
and looks for a way out.

I have now only symbols for grandpa.
I've written myself into and out of moments
like seeing the last light of the sun blooming and reblooming
between trees from the cool open window of an Outback.

Everyone is so loud and everything so soon.
I lean in to my listening, my hand on yours,
and let you know I hear you.
But there is no one here.

4.
What is the function of memory?

I reach over for my glasses and in their place is a tiny version of grandpa
in a tweed suit eating peanuts while wearing the glasses, saying

"I need these more than you do."

When I cry no tears come

but a pressure all over my face.
I do this in secret.

5.
I went to tickle the moon, but it popped and said
"Thank you."

A bipedal horse tromps on the floor above, a party fit for disaster
and applause. And who am I to say anything
about anything—
staring at the floor with my hooves off, applauding.

And how glorious it is to be
anything at all.

THESE DAYS I GROAN LIKE AN OLD OAK WHEN RISING

What roots you
  is a wound
    for me.

    The creek's old hypnosis guides me to my genius,
      where gnats knit a net of guilt in this indigo humidity.
     But still, I will kill them all.

     Mom's gorgeous citrus plants guard the front entrance.
     Water pools from the land's wound, where I stand
     entranced by the summer of that open door.

      The truth is what I want it to be
      a rock in the river.
        It's humans that are alien,

        who demand speech from unspeaking things.
     Close your lips and like a breeze passing
    feel the thoughts and thank them as they go.

    Let things be as they seem.
    Let need flow from being.
    Let the world speak for you.

   It has no need for words.
 I follow my principles into their darkness.
  Noon's eye grills me like a steak.

  Apples of my eyes
  sin orange inversions.
Is this happiness: to be dissolved?

NEW YEAR, 2019: CAPTAIN OF THE SADNESS BOAT

1.
The years and their questionable answers
festoon in the wheeling myrrh
and mirth of mortar soured air.

In nearly every hand,
champagne glasses
clink, clang, tink

their bright effervescences.

Empty minutes bead down
red rimmed flutes, lost in the general
neighborhood clamor. An ambulance

throws its colors on garages, front stair bricks, briefly
on the girl next door whose fitted crimson dress
the breeze chases as she checks her phone

alone on a porch and, finally,
bares its strobe beyond
sight, concern for its wail

absorbed in the uproar.

Driveways are their own pockets of the universe,
where children race with sparklers in time's dilation,
watched by the black rim of the new moon.

How many moons of how many new years
have I proposed fugacious purposes
that a month later I will fail?

I came and have stayed here

under the flimsy pavilion and drunken belief,
surrounded by eruptive laughter and dampening rain,
campfire and confused birdsong,
not knowing the questions I carry.

I bring to my lips the dry and bitter taste of now.
I dig my wet feet into the absolute
necessity of not knowing anything
for another year.

The day is holy in the solitude of this silence.

2.
Last fey hour of 2018.
The moon climbs the night to its zenith.

Gold earrings jangle in their orbits
gilding fear with giddiness.

They glow occasional bronze
from the neighbor's fire, in ersatz ecstacy.

Through wires of opposing Vs,
the gaps of which comprise a fence,

which is the boundary of a suburban life;
bubbly amber champions nervous hands.

Self in glass flute, I am what you conceal.
Here's to dropping the ball on another year.

3.
When does our knowledge catch up to our years?

The loops echo their echoes on a shifting axis,
wheeling and reeling in burning circles.

One cannot tell the dancer from the dance.
A girl twirls dual hoops, center of center.

The rose of the dancing fire blooms.

Explosions in the sky burst their yeses
in accelerating nervousness until
in a lull in the spell, the dull throb of death beats
before the old year's smoldering oblivion.

Hopes swell in the hoops' swoon.
They are a call to motion, and are the image
on which the unreal reconciles the real.

Within minutes all these drooping heads will rest and blossom.
For now, more apocalyptic blasts.

The black dog is a statue of brave confusion.

4.
Cloud dog clover there is no danger,
no works of fire exploding into being.
The war is over.

The day chimes in with noisy clarity.

The ancient suddenness of now opens like a book.
I want to turn the page, and am the page turning.

The initial minutia has faded to a dim clarity
and a faint throb of death in the head.

A season of lilacs opens in the open door
and spring begins its bloom on an open wind.

The wind as wind and nothing more

is like a union of voices that moves us to forgetfulness.

The sun, sunk deep in its wandering, knows no new year.
The hoop dancer enchants her own thoughts, chimerical

miracle, from the black music of winter's wings,
and spins joy of out of the dull bass of January's fire.

Dare I enter the labyrinth of another's being?

The end of my tunnel is the continuation of the tunnel.

Numberless wild geese drift black wild, have awakened
at the end of winter to imagine spring.

I fall open in the provocative mystique of a new year which begins like a poem.

SUMMER NIGHT

I look at the light
the surface of the tree has collected

and overthink everything.

I don't want to be where I am.
And I follow me everywhere I go.

I cradle in the sound of morning
down by the naked field of eternity.

I see the silence
where time scoffs at its name
and disappears
in puffs of space.

Birds peck peepholes
into the night's
awakening roof.

The flashlight wobbles in the dark
finding its place.

I find my place
in that openness,
that space to float in.

I spend half my days indoors.

I think of lions,
guided by Orion
without the need to name.

How much can I observe before I burst
into everything at once?

Here is how the sun burned
its cycle of fire into my bones
like tree rings:

There is the sun
and there is the day.

There is the moon
and there is the night.

The yellow-lashed eye
has finally bobbed
above the mountain's
waves.

Simply,
I exist.

MANY ROACHES DROP FROM A POSTER OF VARIOUS PICTURES OF ME DRESSED AS AN ALIEN

At first it was roaches along the floorboards.
Insects in human suits saying human things,
always at the corner of the eye.
Sometimes you would blow your pursed lips
and I didn't know if you were still you.

When we had sleep overs, I always feared you
would turn into an alien. Into some kind of green goo
and try to take over my body. Hive minds are why
this country scares me.

The roaches crawl out at three.
One night you seemed to float
out of your room into the hall.
I saw you from the moonslant

in the doorway and I felt the way you were feeling
around you without touching anything.
Things crawled along the back of my neck that were never there.
I put my hand on my neck and you were gone from the doorway.
The sun was already on its way up.

Sometimes I don't think for myself.
I drive blind through the day
and say variations of dialogue from movies and the radio.
I tread the same part of the yard drinking the same brand of coffee

out of the same brown ringed mug.
I wake up standing in the doorway.
I go to the forest when I think too much.
I watch all the little creatures carve out their worlds.

I let them crawl on me and bring me into their world.

Like you brought me into yours.
Thank you for teaching me to sleep next to my fears.

THE EYES IN WINDOWPANES

The morning is garlic,
is midnight—
is an elephant's breath
curling down
the dusty particulate air
of the spiral staircase's
hellward march.

In big cities, you tend to imagine
bigger windows.

What we're calling morning is full of slant truth
spilling through upright glass.

It's true, I've not been meeting you
where you're at.

The language is
walking.
The language is
trees.
The language is
a distanceless journey

to what you always were.

There are a few faces around the fire,
so I'll be more specific:

the moon is howling during the day
and no one hears it.

All a day has is its fire
and the moon—

a persistent lullaby.

There is truth and there is what I am calling truth.
I can meet you there.

You'll run back to the fire that licked you,
weeping ashes from your eyes.

You'll make an idol of whoever rebukes you,
looking to occupy your idle hands.

Your deflections will bury you.
Blue coffin of the world, I have buried us.

Come, pick up your grave and carry it.

I've been speaking my language
and expecting you to know it.

Clouds in passing make shadows on the ground,
which could be the language you need.

If you have to manhandle your emotions
to present as peaceful,
I have some thoughts for you.

I will hold on to them.

What do I know of grief?

You're right.
and I am here beside you.

FLICKING ASHES OFF THE PIER

Behind the nimbus hanging
over this gun metal New York night,
the pomegranate in Hades' ghastly grasp
flecks gridded shadows through gridiron streets. Sunset.
No hedons. No heathens. Just disco
striations flaring up the Eastern skyline.

Drowning Cerberus claws at the shore
where we climbed the misty lights
of the shutdown ferris wheel,
went swimming in our dress shoes, where Daddy
beat the Atlantic sand out of our skin.

One early morning, with the nightmare
hour pressing me down,
I saw an orb of light the size of a small fruit
hover an inch above the floor and slowly
float into my parent's room.
The next day, my brother and I at breakfast
shared a look, where we both nodded at each other,
then tripped back up to our rooms.

Daddy fades in and out of these memories like a fever phantom.
Sometimes he dissolves like an Alka-Seltzer.
I remember his face mostly as other men's faces.

His wild eyes once stunned me enough to join him
on a drive to his young girlfriend's house
while he smoked a joint. He doused the outside
of her apartment in kerosene and prayed
her house into a conflagration
with upward swoops of his arms.
I looked back in a morbid need to know
and between his fingers, the orb of light
surrounding the match almost lit a fire in me.

Daddy hides glowing seeds in his fist,
each pulse of its densest starlight
threatening to suck me into its orbit.

This blood orange sun is a grapefruit I'm carving
so I may sneak inside and sleep.

A wet dress shoe's gloss catches the moon
walking on a floor of waves.

The distant wheel is an eye of light
in the shadow of the pier, spinning
against the world's spinning. Moon
glaring in wheel's steel, tire's rubber
burns and turns, scattering sand,
speeding away from the salty hiss
and rolling back home to mother,
while the glare of his cigarette flares
in the metal of the seatbelt I click,
one half of me clothed,
the other floating somewhere in the Atlantic.

The wind under the water carries the memories further out to sea.

I. SHADOW PEOPLE

You wake and don't call yourself a monster.
The monsters under your bed are grateful.
The human shapes at your bedside are grateful.
There is truth in the darkness.
There's truth and belief.
We've talked about this before.

Brother, I believe you.

I will not walk the same path as you
both by choice and necessity.

But we wear the same shadow.

As an act of self-care,
I'm going to stop talking.

I'm going to sleep
in the curl of the moon.

Goodnight, words.

We are not doomed
to repeat the choices of those who came before us.

We are not doomed
to repeat the choices of those who came before us.

II. SHADOW WORK

A sequence unfolds from its networks.
Suppose an object craves its subject: cages in search of birds.
Suppose then, a shadow seeks its origin
to better know itself.

Your bones made my bones
is a line that keeps haunting this poem.

It's nice. But it's not truth.

I am what my father lacked.

If you think there is triumph in this
and that it sounds sad at the same time,
yes.
I have fathered a self out of an absence
and said yes to lack.
Only then have I flown through the lack in my sleep
to dream my now.
I know my now as a feeling.
No deep and abiding peace, clouds, a light blue forever,
no zero meadow with the one mother tree. There is no poetry
in the nameless feeling.
It springs up one word by one word.
So often we say "I feel", then state a thought.
I believe "it" starts with how we speak to ourselves.
I love you and care for your time,
and I must go now
to speak to myself.

Is your heart at war or at peace?

III. THE TRUEST REALITY IS THE IMAGINATION

I'm learning to live with the shadow people
at the edge of the bed and their indigo energy,
which is teaching me to live with less judgment.

Some days are clouds above my head.
Some clouds are days-wide.

Have I grown too swiftly to accept myself?
Language collapses into words.

Words into letters. Letters into blots of ink.
Time grows precious.

Afternoons disintegrate into a distance I can walk to meet you.
This moment will be a memory.

Memory as vision without seeing.
Seeing as vision without memory.

There is the other plane
and there is what we call the other plane.

Here, you are bound by your belief of freedom,
which has collapsed reality into an idea.

We are not bound by the world
but by our choices in the world

we call reality.
We are not even bound to a single life.

Brother, our rage takes the shape of a child in an attic.
Who convinced that child that scars need to heal?

DRIVING WEST

1.
Staring at the starred abyss,
people are passing us in the left lane.
The asphalt is glazed by the sun's watching,
like the watch on my father's other son's wrist.
I don't remember much outside of the car's box.
I don't remember the objects in the car,
our little world. Our bodies were an extension of the car.
I recall feeling like we rented our lives year by year.
Every year a new beige car.

2
You've felt it calling,
felt the wheels spin toward it
when the rest of your family slept
or seemed like extensions of the car.
But you were an abstraction beyond the car.
The car was your companion.
The road was the car's companion.
Time is a breeze that doesn't move air.
And the air shakes everything westward.
The moon is trivial and the cactus is everything.
Amid the whir and chirp of night's dilation,
pine trees stand nude and skeletal
in winter's white deletion.
You stand outside the car and evening
touches the world into one shadow.
This merge of years is you.

ORANGE CIRCLES OPEN TO A BIGGER ORANGE CIRCLE

Low tide's denim cuffs my ankles,
rolls like fields of purple heath in memory's wind
where I seek peace from time in the lilac breeze
of another country and time.

Red and brown leaves whirl in the swirl
of the world winding up. Cool water runs soundless
under sun in memory of the russet stream
where iron ore's rusted bronze history glints.
Dawn's alchemy sparks behind cumulus drifts,
leaves' burnt flirtings flick like chapters
of a book on occultism.

These were the dark and evil days of sleep—black sleep
that tied loose ends of days together
then took the days entirely and gave them
to a changing cast of faceless heads speaking
awful gibberish I was sure was about me.
Each day was each blue wave
breaking its head upon the next.

In the blue-bleak mornings I'd watch the world
from a window or a street as people retreated
from rain. And what am I trying to say?
The wind leaned saplings into the sun
and they looked like candlesticks in the wide green
where the black lion loomed.

In the cold courtyard under the noon sun,
the others lay soundless like trees
or individual moments. I plucked flowers
Puck-like to plant in their eyes
and built a steady foundation of
"everything is fine."

I embrace you in the thunder
of this time's tide that pulls your hair down
your skull, younger me, and forgive you by pushing you
out to the mind's sea like a newborn.
A flower for your eyes?

LEAVING THE OVEN ON

Your nervous system like an ancient tree lights up and sucks its breath inside you. From the window you imagine a grey river in the vision of a wilderness of mirrors. You hear the phone and are pulled from this reflection. Ringing and ringing, ripples spread out from the center. Disembodied legs feel the wind under the water. Shored reeds sway in the imagined river's unseen breeze, you imagine. The porch light flickers like a neuron's unprovoked twitch. The burl of the whispering tree does not eye you in your defenseless saunter. The squirrel in the tree across the street must return to his stash in the arbor hollow, and the secret you stashed away will be found. Everyone knows it. The shadow of the sycamore looms over the mauve gloom of its leaves' shadows caught and clawing at the stairs.

ARRIVING SOMEWHERE

The wilderness in the middle of your life sports a hotel.
The concierge is taking a smoke break outside, legs up on the table.

He will say "self care or community" and you will say
"I got this" while screaming internally because asking for help
might be a slight inconvenience to a stranger.

You will trade twelve impeccable words with your boss
after practicing an hour.

You will lay away your day off.

Eventually, you will get up for a shower
because it's not worth it.

You've got a lot of debt and also that piece of paper,
so you will make some water at a temperature.

Wine and candles.

As you light them, the shadow your hand casts
will invade your nothing.

You will want to feel a hand in the dark,
but you won't know how to say that.

SITTING AMONG SYCAMORES, OUTSIDE OF TIME

Soft rain. The woods knuckle.
Trees hold up the sky. So many
ways of saying hello to silence.
Bearded oaks and mossy
stumps. Snakes and / or
vines. A wet shimmer over all things.
Red pixel of distant fire, yellow eyes of a truck.
Wind of different voices. The shimmering dark.
More stars every blink.

What can I say that hasn't been said before?

CHARLIE

They planted Robert near his favorite golf course.
Grandpa and granddad had already been taken, so Robert.

I have an egg carton of golf balls he collected
from the same course where he also participated
in ornithology, or: looking at the sky and hurting one's neck.

The sun's feathered rays alight
to witness the earth, hence clouds
for privacy.

Grandpa
was the one who grew colder and colder
in the rocking chair he made
until his soul seeped out
and now chills his favorite corners of that house to 66 degrees.

When I was born twenty days early for a soul,
someone forgot to give me a mission. What I mean is
I am grateful for what I'm missing.

The big E used to look like a triangle
and now it's not there at all.

Birds are flowers or leaves at a certain distance
and, eventually, cold stones.

I'm not sure if the drops counteract cataracts, glaucoma,
or whatever it is this week. The truth is

two words I've learned to be resistant to.
But hear me out: dawn forever, unlimited dogs.

My pirate dog, when freed out of the shell of his home
into the cold of the blue morning,

performs a canine cursive of several turns
and returns a few feet from his original spot.

Mom hasn't oiled the door hinge to the porch screen
because he needs to hear it to come inside.

One must open it three times so he can circle
and decide it's safe to come in.

It's safe to come in.

VAGUE APPROXIMATIONS OF THINGS OTHER PEOPLE HAVE SAID BEFORE AND IN BETTER WAYS

The curse is that you will still look for love
long after you've found it.
I can touch your void with mine.

Because nothing is ever actually
touching another thing.
Let us deconstruct

each other's deconstructions.
But O,
where is the heart?

It's empty in here,
but here are some words.
Pure being is only an instant of meaning.

It is not the person that is dead due to sleeping,
it is the life since its inception.
It is a dead life.

What has passed is what is.
The real man that you want doesn't exist.
Here I am, though.

With a bit too much hair and a bit too lean of frame
to be an archetype.
Have you read the magazine:

Another White Boy Is Sad For No Reason: The Daddy Issue?
Old as I am still young, my void is an inner room.
There is a bunk bed and a Super Nintendo

and I am going to close the door now.

ACKNOWLEDGMENTS

Ghost City Review: "You're Hunting for Unicorns at the Bar When Jack London Walks In"
Riggwelter Press: "Eating Breakfast"

And Sometimes Why, a chapbook containing several of these poems, was published by Zoetic Press in June 2019.

ABOUT THE AUTHOR

Daniel Warner was born in Augusta, Ga. He is the author of *Shadow Work* as well as the chapbooks *Woke* and *And Sometimes Why*. He was a finalist in the 2018 Wergle Flomp Poetry Contest, and his poetry has been featured in Rust + Moth, Pretty Owl Poetry, and elsewhere. He has received scholarships for the Prague Summer Program for Writers, Winter Tangerine Review's Online Workshop, and the Adroit Journal's Summer Mentorship Program. He lives around Atlanta, Ga, and likes dogs better.